In the name of God

Easy reading based on concordle-cloud

Azadeh Nemati (Ph.D)
Marjan Khoshparvar (M.A)

Jungle Publication

Significance of the book

Reading and vocabulary are two important aspects of language. Though different methods were used in class students are not still strong in these areas. By using concorancing and word clouding in class to teach reading comprehendion and vocabulary this book is going to shed some light. A lot of work is done in the realm of vocabulary and comprehension but concorlde is a new method that is useful in teaching.

It is recommended that teachers show concordle cloud of the related units to the students before starting reading and then proceed to teach.

Table of Contents

Significance of the book iii
New Shoes 1
A Thin Man 3
Buy a New Car 5
Cold Weather 7
Love 9
Piano Player 11
A Fast Driver 13
A Clean Floor 15
News Every Day 17
Earthquake 19
A Beautiful Jacket 21
A Lot of Cash 23
Let's Go Fishing 25
A Mountain Drive 27
The Phone Call 29
A New Baby 31
Eat Like a Wolf 33
About the authors 35

pair ^{different} ^{always}

^{loves} shoes^{mile} shopping
^{just} ^{might}
lisa ^{pairs} she ^{price} tomorrow^{from}
^{new} ^{pretty} ^{four}
^{house} mall^{needs} will
^{has} ^{minutes}
buy ^{good}
^{going}

New Shoes

Lisa loves to go shopping. Tomorrow she is going shopping. She needs a new **pair** of shoes. She wants to buy a pair of red shoes. She thinks red shoes are **pretty**. She will buy a pair of shoes at the **mall**. Lisa usually shops at the mall. The mall is only a mile from her house. She just walks to the mall. It only takes her 20 minutes. Tomorrow she will go to four different shoe **stores**. Tomorrow is Saturday. The mall always has sales on Saturday. If the sale price is good, Lisa might buy two pairs of shoes.

Pair: joined together, an object that is made from two similar parts that are joined together.
Ex. Pair of shoes, pair of jeans, pair of scissors etc.

.**Pretty:** Beautiful
.**Mall:** Shopping centre
.**Store:** Shop
.**Price:** The amount of money you have to pay for something
*New # Old
*Buy# Sell
*Good# Bad

EASY READING BASED ON CONCORDLE-CLOUD   1

Answer the following questions:
1. What does Lisa need?
   a. a pair of jeans   b. a pair of shoes
   c. a bag   d. a pencil case
2. How does she go to the mall?
   a. She goes by taxi   b. She goes by bus
   c. She walks to the mall   d. She goes by bicycle
3. What day is tomorrow?
   a. Saturday   b. Tuesday
   c. Sunday   d. Monday

Fill in the blank.
1. Tomorrow Lisa is going ……………….
2. She thinks ………. Shoes are pretty.
3. She will buy a pair of shoes at the ………...
4. Tomorrow is ……………. .
5. If the sale price is good, she might buy ……….. pairs of …………. .

Matching.

.Pretty	.Bad
.Store	.Beautiful
. New#	.Shop
. Good#	.Old

^{always}
^{all}

light

^{get}_{eat} **eats** ^{isnt}_{heavy} **eater**

for^{doesnt}_{because}

A Thin Man

Richard is a **light eater**. He doesn't eat much. He isn't a heavy eater. He eats a light **breakfast**, a light **lunch**, and a light **dinner**. Richard is not fat. He is thin. He will always be thin, because he is a light eater. He eats a **bowl** of cereal for breakfast. He eats a bowl of cereal with milk. He eats a sandwich for lunch. Sometimes it's a fish sandwich. He likes fish. He eats rice and vegetables for dinner. All he eats for dinner is rice and vegetables. He will never get fat.

.Light: Little, few
. Eater: Someone who eats something
.Breakfast: The meal you have in the morning
.Lunch: A meal eaten in the middle of the day
. Dinner: the meal you have in the evening or at night
.Bowl: Dish

*Light# Heavy
*Thin# Fat

EASY READING BASED ON CONCORDLE-CLOUD   3

Answer the following questions:
1. What does Richard look like?
   a. He is fat.   b. He is tall.
   c. He is short.   d. He is thin.
2. What does he eat for his breakfast?
   a. He eats fish sandwich   b. He eats rice.
   c. He eats vegetables.   d. He eats cereal with milk
3. What does he eat for his lunch?
   a. Rice and Milk   b. Vegetables
   c. fish sandwich   d. fish and vegetables

Fill in the blank.
1. Richard is a ……… eater.
2. He eats ………… and ……….. for dinner.
3. Richard is a ………. Man.
4. He eats cereal with……….
5. He eats sandwich for……….

Matching.
.Fat   .Dish
.Bowl   .Thin
.Light   .Heavy

linda

Buy a New Car

Linda wants to buy a new car. She has an old car. Her old car is a white Honda. Linda wants to buy a new Honda. She wants to buy a new red Honda. She has **saved** $1,000. She will use $1,000 to help buy the new car. She will give $1,000 to the Honda **dealer**. The Honda dealer will give her a **contract** to **sign**. The contract will **require** her to pay $400 a month for seven years. Her new red Honda will **cost** Linda a **lot** of money. But that's okay, because Linda makes a lot of money.

- **.Save:** To keep money in a bank so that you can use it later
- **.Dealer:** Someone who buys and sells a product, specially an expensive one
- **EX.** Car, art, etc.
- **.Contract:** An official agreement between two or more people
- **.Sign:** A shape that it is particular for each person
- **.Require:** Need
- **.Cost:** The amount of money that you have to pay in order to buy something
- **.Lot:** A large number

Answer the following questions:
1. What does Linda want to buy?
   a. She wants to buy a new house
   b. She wants to buy a new car
   c. She wants to buy a new shop
   d. She wants to buy a new washing machine
2. How much she will give to Honda dealer?
   a. $2000   b. $3000
   c. $ 400   d. $ 1000
3. What color is her old Honda?
   a. Blue   b. Green
   c. White   d. Red

Fill in the blank.
1. Linda wants to buy a new ....
2. She has saved ....
3. The Honda dealer will give her a .... to sign.
4. Linda makes a lot of ....
5. She will give $1000 to ....

Matching.
.Require   .Need
.Dealer   .Large number
.Lot   .A person who buys and sells a product

```
              for
                                    closed
                      either       looked
                                                      hot
                    warm      not                     his
          door                                                        put
                        found            none
                  jacket  did  was       like    were   open
                    thomas
                                   cold         weather     warmer
                    all         windows            still
                                  they            wasnt
                                   yes
```

Cold Weather

Thomas was not **hot**. He was not **warm** either. He was cold. The weather was not hot. The weather was not warm either. The weather was cold. Thomas did not like to be cold. He **looked for** his jacket. He found his jacket. He **put on** his jacket. But he was still cold. He looked at the windows. Were all the windows closed? Yes, they were. They were all closed. None of the windows were open. He looked at the door. The door wasn't open. It was closed. He was still cold. He looked for a warmer jacket.

.**Hot:**   High temperature
.**Warm:**   Comfortable temperature, cool
.**Look for:** Search for
.**Put on:** wear
*Hot# Cold
*Open# Close

Answer the following questions:
1. How was the weather?
   a. Cold   b. Hot
   c. Warm   d. Windy
2. What did Thomas look for?
   a. He looked for his shoes   b. He looked for his Jacket
   c. He looked for his umbrella   d. He looked for his hat
3. Were all the windows closed?
   a. Yes, they were.   b. No, they were not.
   c. Yes, they are.   d. No, they aren't

Fill in the blanks.
1. Thomas was ………..
2. He………………….. his jacket.
3. None of the ……………were open.
4. He looked for a warmer ………….
5. The door wasn't …………….

Matching.
.Hot   .Close
.Open   .Wear
.Look for   .Cold
.Put on   .Search for

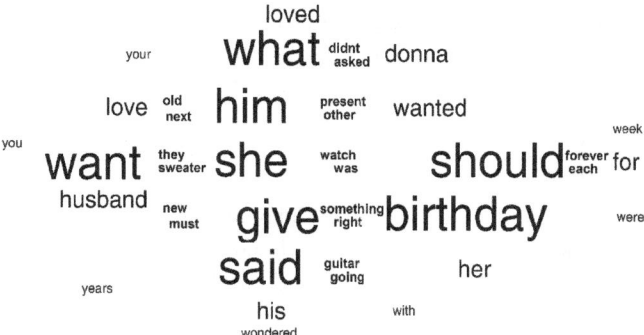

Love

Donna loved her husband. Her husband loved Donna. They were in love with each other. She wanted to give him a birthday **present**. He was going to be 40 years old next week. She **wondered** what to give him. Should she give him a watch? Should she give him a **sweater**? Should she give him a new guitar? What should she give him? She asked him what he wanted for his birthday. He said he didn't want anything for his birthday. "Oh, you must want something!" she said. "You're right," he said. "I want your love **forever**."

.**Present:** Gift
.**Wonder:** To think about something that you are not sure about
.**Sweater:** Jumper
.**Forever:** For all future time

Answer the following questions:
1. What did she want to give him?
   a. Car b. Birthday present
   c. Guitar d. Sweater
2. How old was he going to be?
   a. 35 years old b. 45 years old
   c. 40 years old d. 50 years old
3. What did he want for his birthday present?
   a. Sweater b. Guitar
   c. Watch d. her love forever

Fill in the blanks.
1. Donna loved her …………..
2. Donna and her husband were in love with …………………..
3. She………….what to give him.
4. He was going to be………………… Next week.
5. He said" I want……………………………….. ".

Matching.
.Present   .Jumper
.sweater   .Gift
.Forever   .For all the future time

his

hands **piano** loves
four   living

has eyes big

Piano Player

Donald plays the piano. He loves the piano. He has a big piano in his living room. His piano is **shiny** and black. It has three legs. He sits on a **bench** to play the piano. The bench has four legs. His piano has 88 keys. The keys are black and white. Donald has ten fingers. His ten fingers play music on the 88 piano keys. The piano also has three **pedals**. Donald uses his two feet on the three pedals. He uses both of his hands and both of his feet to play the piano. He also uses both of his eyes to play the piano.

.**Shiny:** Bright
.**Bench:** Long seat

.**Pedal:** A part on piano that you press with your feet to change the quality of the sound
***Big# Small**

Answer the following questions:
1. What does Donald play?
   a. Guitar   b. violin
   c. drum   d. piano
2. How many keys does piano have?
   a. The piano has 88 keys   b. The piano has 188 keys
   c. The piano has 100 keys   d. The piano has 10 keys
3. How many fingers does he have?
   a. 20   b. 88
   c. 10   d. 3

Fill in the blanks.
1. He sits on the ………… to play the piano.
2. The keys are……….. and ………….
3. His ……. Fingers play ……….. on the 88 piano keys.
4. The piano has three …………….
5. He uses both of his ………….. and both of his…………. To play the piano.

Matching.
.Pedal   .Big
.Bench   .Bright
.Small   .Long seat
.Shiny   .A part in piano you push with your feet

A Fast Driver

Brian has a **fast** car. He drives his car fast. He never gets a **ticket**. His car is too fast for the police. They **chase** him, but they can't **catch** him. Brian always **escapes** from the police. The police want to catch him. But their cars are too **slow**. Brian's car is very fast. He likes to drive over 100 **mph**. When he sees the police, he waves to the police. The police turn on their **sirens**. They turn on their red lights. They chase after Brian. Brian speeds up. He passes all the other cars on the road. He escapes from the police.

- **.Fast:** Moving quickly
- **.Ticket:** A printed piece of paper
- **.Chase:** To quickly follow someone or something
- **.Catch:** To suddenly take hold of someone or something
- **.Escape:** To get away from a dangerous or bad situation
- **.Slow:** Not quick, not moving
- **.mph:** Miles per hour, used to describe the speed of something
- **.Siren:** A piece of equipment that makes very loud warning sounds, used for police cars, ambulances, etc.

*Fast# Slow

Answer the following questions:
1. How Brian drive his car?
   a. He drives slowly   b. He drives fast
   c. He drives carefully   d. He drives carelessly
2. Can the police catch him?
   a. Yes, they can   b. No, they can't
   c. Yes, they do   d. No, they don't
3. Does he escape from the police?
   a. No, he doesn't. He drives slowly
   b. Yes, he does. He drives fast
   c. No, he doesn't. He gets a ticket
   d. Yes he does. He runs fast

Fill in the blank.
1. Brian never gets a ....
2. He likes to drive over ....mph.
3. The police .... The siren.
4. When he sees the police, he .... to them.
5. .... want to catch Brain.

Matching.
.Fast   .Not quick
.Siren   .Hold some one
.Slow   .Quick
.Ticket   .A piece of paper
.Catch   .An equipment with loud sound

pieces broom/all

his/eat saw like/into kitchen

little dirty/didnt

A Clean Floor

Ed looked at the **kitchen** floor. The kitchen floor was **dirty**. There were little pieces of food on the floor. Ed saw bread **crumbs**. He saw **cracker** crumbs. He saw **cheese** crumbs. He saw little pieces of bread. He saw little pieces of cracker. He saw little pieces of cheese. He needed to **sweep** the floor. Ed didn't want **bugs** in his kitchen. Bugs like to eat little pieces of food. He took the **broom** out of the kitchen closet. He took the **dust pan** out of the kitchen closet. Ed swept the floor. He swept all the pieces of food into the dust pan.

- **.Kitchen:** A room where you prepare and cook food
- **.Dirty:** Not clean
- **.Crumb:** A very small piece of dry food, like bread or cake
- **.Cracker:** A hard dry type of bread

- **.Cheese:** Solid food made from milk

- **.Sweep:** Clean something
- **.Bug:** A small insect
- **.Broom:** A large brush with a long handle, used for sweeping floor

.Dust pan: A flat container with a handle that you use with a brush to remove dust from the floor

*Dirty# Clean

Answer the following questions:
1. How was the kitchen floor?
   a. Clean   b. Shiny
   c. Dirty   d. Wet
2. What do bugs like to eat?
   a. Milk   b. water
   c. cheese   d. little pieces of food
3. What did Ed see in the kitchen?
   a. He saw bugs   b. He saw dustpan
   c. He saw a glass of juice   d. He saw little pieces of food

Fill in the blank.
1. The kitchen floor was ……………..
2. He …………….. the floor with broom and dust pan.
3. There were little pieces of…………. On the …………….
4. He saw crackers……………. on the floor.
5. He took the ……………….out of the kitchen closet.

Matching.
.Dirty   .Not clean
.Sweep   .Clean
.Bug   .A room you cook food there
.Kitchen   .Insect

_{city} **she** _{everyone}
_{but}   _{country}

_{interesting} **news** _{knows}   there
_{why} _{has}   _{isnt}

_{because}   **every**^{good}
_{bad}   ^{fresh}
         _{usually}   _{answer}
                      _{all}

News Every Day

Jackie loves the **news**. She listens to the news on the radio. She watches the news on TV. She reads the news in the **newspaper**. She reads the news in **magazines**. She loves the news because it is always new. It is always **fresh**. It is always **interesting**. There is news every day. There is news in every country. There is news in every state. There is news in every city. Everyone all over the **world** talks about the news every day. But Jackie has a question about the news. Why is the news usually bad? Why isn't the news usually good? No one knows the answer.

- **.News:** Information about something that has happened recently
- **.Newspaper:** A set a large folded sheets of printed paper containing news, articles, pictures, advertisements, etc.

- **.Magazine:** A large thin book with a paper cover that contains new stories, articles, photographs etc, and is sold weekly or monthly

- **.Fresh:** New
- **.Interesting:** If something is interesting, you give it your attention

.**World:** Universe
***Fresh# Old**
***Interesting# Boring**
***Good# Bad**

Answer the following questions:
1. What does Jackie love?
   a. Music   b. News
   c. Films   d. Books
2. Is the news boring for Jackie?
   a. Yes, it is   b. No, it isn't
   c. Yes, it does   d. No, it doesn't
3. How she has gotten news?
   a. Read newspaper   b. watch TV and Listen to music
   c. Read short stories d. read newspaper and listen to the radio

Fill in the blank.
1. She ………………….. the news in newspaper.
2. Jackie reads …………………in magazines.
3. Every all over the …………..talks about the news every day.
4. …………………..is always interesting.
5. She watches the news on ………..

Matching.
.Fresh   .Good
.Interesting   .Universe
.Bad   .Boring
.World   .Old

Earthquake

Michelle felt the **earthquake**. It lasted for only five seconds. The whole house **shook**. She heard noise. The TV went off. The lights went off. She was **scared**. She had never felt an earthquake. It was very **strong**. It was as if a **giant** hand had shaken her house. The lights came back on. Michelle turned the TV on. The TV had no news about the earthquake. She turned on the radio. The radio said it was a 4.7 earthquake. But there was no **damage**. No one was **hurt**. Everyone was okay. No houses had damage. Everything was okay. But Michelle was still scared. She wanted to move far away. She did not like earthquakes. They were so **scary**.

.**Earthquake:** A sudden shaking of the earth's surface that often causes a lot of damage
.**Shake:** Move
.**Scared:** Afraid
.**Strong:** Not weak
.**Giant:** Very big
.**Damage:** Harm
.**Hurt:** Injure
.**Scary:** Frightening

Answer the following questions:
1. What did Michelle feel?
   a. Pain　　　　　　　　b. Cold
   c. Heat　　　　　　　　d. earthquake
2. How was the strength of earthquake?
   a. 4.6　　　　　　　　b. 4.7
   c. 5.4　　　　　　　　d. 7.4
3. Was she happy?
   a. Yes, she was. She was happy
   b. No, she wasn't. She was sad
   c. No, she wasn't. She was scared
   d. No, she wasn't. she was nervous

Fill in the blank.
1. The earthquake lasted for only……………….
2. The TV had no ………….. about the earthquake.
3. No one was …………….
4. The radio said it was a ……….earthquake.
5. She wanted to move………….

Matching.
.Giant　　　　　　　　.Afraid
.Strong　　　　　　　.Very big
.Scared　　　　　　　.Not weak

A Beautiful Jacket

He loved his new jacket. It was his **favorite** jacket. He loved the color. It was **tan**. He loved the **weight.** It was medium weight. It was not too **light**. It was not too heavy. He loved the **fit**. It fit him **well**. He put the jacket on. He looked at the jacket in the **mirror**. It looked good. What a good-looking jacket, he thought. He went to the doctor's office. The office was warm. He took his jacket off. He put it on the chair next to him. A nurse called his name. He stood up. He went to the **examination room**. He forgot that his jacket was on the chair. But it wasn't on the chair for long. Another **patient** took it home.

.**Favorite:** Your favorite person or thing is the one that you like the most
.**Tan:** Brown and yellow
.**Weight:** something that is heavy
.**Light:** Not heavy

.Fit: If a piece of clothing fits you, it is the right size for your body
.Well: ok
.Mirror: A piece of special glass that you can look at and see yourself in
.Examination room: A room that sets of medical tests
.Patient: Sick
*New*Old
*Put on# Take off
*Heavy# Light

Answer the following questions:
1. What color is the jacket?
   a. Blue   b. Brown
   c. Tan   d. Green
2. Where did he go?
   a. He went to cinema   b. He went to factory
   c. He went to Hospital   d. He went to doctor's office
3. How was the weather in the doctor's office?
   a. Warm   b. Hot
   c. Cold   d. Cool

Fill in the blank.
1. The jacket fit him ……….
2. He looked at the jacket in the……………..
3. He went to the………………………
4. He forgot that his ……………..was on the chair.
5. Another ……………..took the jacket home.

Matching.
.Patient   .Sick
.Light   .Brown and yellow
.Fit   .Ok
.Tan   .Size
.Well   .Not heavy

A Lot of Cash

She was sitting in a **park**. She started to talk. She started to talk too much. She talked about her **cash**. She talked about a lot of cash. She had thousands of dollars in her purse. She said she had $20,000 in her purse. She said it out loud. Everyone in the place heard her. Everyone looked at her. She took some cash out of her purse. She held the money in the air. "Look," she said, "here's $1,000 cash." She **waved** it around. She laughed. She put the money back in her purse. She had another tea. A man was watching her. She finished her tea. She left the place. He followed her.

.**Cash:**   Money
.**Wave:**   Move

Answer the following questions:
1. Where was she?
   a. Place   b. Park
   c. At work   d. Restaurant
2. How many dollars did she have?
   a. She had $30,0000   b. She had $200,000
   c. She had $20,000   d. She had $45,0000
3. What was she drink?
   a. She drank tea   b. She drank coffee
   c. She drank milk   d. She drank water

Fill in the blank.
1. She was drinking tea so she was getting ………………. .
2. She talked about her …………. .
3. She held ……………..in the air.
4. She had $20,000 in her……………. .
5. She was sitting in……………… .

Matching.
.Wave   .Money
.Drunk   .Move
.Cash   .Unconscious

Let's Go Fishing

They walked onto the dock. They got into the **boat**. They had all their fishing **gear**. They were going fishing. They loved to go fishing. Sometimes they caught a lot of fish. Sometimes they caught a couple of fish. Sometimes they caught no fish. But fishing was fun even if they caught no fish. The boat left the dock. The boat stopped in the middle of the lake. Everyone put worms on their **hooks**. Some people put live worms on their hooks. Some people put dead worms on their hooks. Some people put **rubber** worms on their hooks. Everyone **dropped** their hooks into the water. Then they waited. They waited for the fish to **bite** the worms.

.**Boat:** A vehicle that travels across water

.**Gear:** A set of equipment or tools you need for particular activity

.**Hook:** A curved piece of thin metal with a sharp point for catching fish

.**Rubber:** Forged
.**Drop:** To fall
.**Bite:** To use your teeth to cut

EASY READING BASED ON CONCORDLE-CLOUD

Answer the following questions:
1. Where were they going?
   a. They were going swimming
   b. They were going hiking
   c. They were going fishing
   d. They were going camping
2. What did they put on their hooks?
   a. They put meals on their hooks
   b. They put crumb on their hooks
   c. They put chicken on their hooks
   d. They put worms on their hooks
3. What did they love?
   a. They loved to go hiking   b They loved to go swimming
   c. They loved to go camping   d. They loved to go fishing

Fill in the blank.
1. They walk onto the ………..
2. They loved to go to ………………..
3. The boat stopped in the…………..of the……………….
4. Everyone put worms on their ……………..
5. Some people put ………….. worms on their hooks.

Matching.
.Bite	.Cut something with your teeth
.Drop	.A piece of thin metal for catching fish
.Hook	.To fall

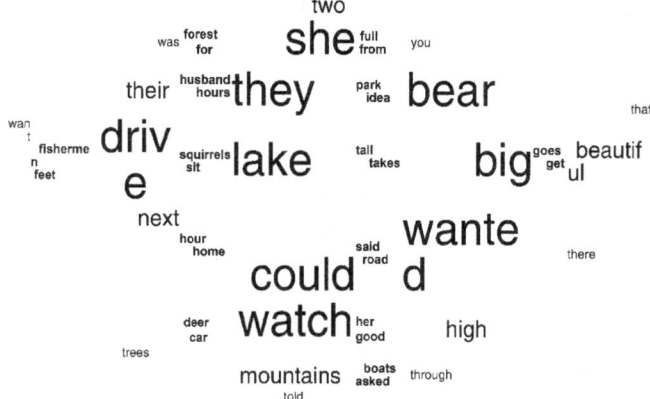

A Mountain Drive

She wanted to go for a drive. She told her husband. He said that was a good idea. "Where do you want to go?" he asked. She wanted to drive to the **mountains.** She wanted to go to Big Bear **Lake**. Big Bear Lake is high in the mountains. It is 7,000 feet high. It is a two-hour drive from their home. It takes two hours to get there. The lake is big and beautiful. They could park their car next to the lake. They could sit next to the lake. They could watch the boats. They could watch the **fishermen**. They could watch the **squirrels** and **deer**. It is a beautiful drive to Big Bear Lake. The road goes through a big **forest** full of tall trees.

.Mountain: A very high hill

.Lake: A large area of water surrounded by land

.Fisherman: Someone who catches fish as a sport or as a job
.Squirrel: A small animal with long furry tail that climbs trees and eats nuts

.Deer: A large wild animal that can run very fast, eats grass, and has horns

.Forest: Jungle

Answer the following questions:
1. Where did she want to go?
   a. Hiking   b. fishing   c. driving   d. camping
2. How high is the mountain?
   a. It is 7,000 feet high   b. It is 4,000 feet high
   c. It is 3,000 feet high   d. It is 7500 feet high
3. Where could they park the car?
   a. Next to the lake   b. Behind the lake
   c. Next to the forest   d. next to the mountain.

Fill in the blank.
1. She told her……………
2. She wanted to drive to ……………
3. It takes …………to get there.
4. They could sit next to the……….
5. The road goes through a big ……………full of ………….

Matching.

.Fisherman	.Jungle
.Mountain	.A large area of water
.Forest	.A person who catches fish
.Lake	. A very high hill

The Phone Call

The phone rang as he was leaving the apartment. He didn't answer it. It's **probably** Dave, he thought. His brother Dave had said he would call. He returned home an hour later. He checked his phone for missed calls. There was only the one call. But it wasn't his brother's number. Who could it be, he **wondered**. He **dialed** the number. A woman answered. She said, "Hello, Kim, how are you doing?" Kim was his wife's name. Who is this, he wondered. "Who's this?" he asked. "Who's this?" she asked. "You called me." He didn't answer. Now he **realized** who it was. It was some woman who called his wife **occasionally**. They had been **classmates** at school. His wife was **polite** to her. But his wife didn't like her. She never returned this woman's phone calls. He himself had never met or talked to her. "Sorry, **wrong** number," he said.

.**Probably:** Used to say something is likely to happen
.**Wonder:** To feel surprised and unable to believe
.**Dial:** Press key's telephone number to make a call
.**Realize:** Understand
.**Occasionally:** Sometimes
.**Classmate:** A member of the same class in a school
.**Polite:** Behaving or speaking in a way that is correct for the social situation you are in, Not rude
.**Wrong:** Not correct
*Polite# Rude / Impolite
* Wrong# Right

Answer the following questions:
1. Who is Kim?
   a. His Mother
   b. His Wife
   c. His Sister
   d. His Friend
2. Who was call?
   a. His Brother
   b. His Wife
   c. His wife's classmate
   d. His Classmate
3. Did Kim like her friend?
   a. Yes, She did
   b. No, she didn't
   c. Yes, she was
   d. No , She wasn't

Fill in the blank.
1. The phone rang as he was leaving ………………………
2. He checked his phone for ………………
3. The woman was Kim's ……………at school.
4. Kim is ………………to her.
5. He …………..never talked to her.

Matching.
.Realize   .Sometimes
.Polite   .Not correct
.Classmate   .Understand
.Wrong   .Not rude

A New Baby

Ruth is **pregnant**. She is expecting a baby. The baby is due in two months. The baby is a boy. It is her first boy. She already has a little girl. Her little girl is two years old. Ruth loves her little girl. Her little girl is happy to get a baby brother. Ruth is eating for two people right now. She is very **careful** about what she eats and drinks. She eats a lot of fresh fruits and vegetables. She eats fresh fish twice a week. She doesn't drink tea or coffee. She doesn't eat **candy** or potato chips. She stays away from cigarette **smokers**. She will have a **healthy** baby.

- **.Pregnant:** If a woman is pregnant, she has an unborn baby growing inside her body
- **.Careful:** Trying very hard to avoid doing anything wrong
- **.Candy:** A sweet food made from sugar or chocolate
- **.Smoker:** Someone who smokes cigarettes
- **.Healthy:** Physically strong

*Careful# Careless

Answer the following questions:
1. How many children does Ruth have?
    a. One girl
    b. Two boys
    c. One boy
    d. four girls
2. What does she eat?
    a. Candy and fruits
    b. Potato chips and vegetables
    c. Candy and Vegetables
    d. Fish and fruits
3. How old is her baby?
    a. Three months
    b. Six months
    c. Two months
    d. Eight months

Fill in the blank.
1. Ruth is…………….
2. She is very …………….about what she eats and drinks.
3. She doesn't eat………………. and …………………..
4. She stays away from ……………………………….
5. She will have a ………… baby.

Matching.

.Candy .A person who smokes cigarette
.Smoker .A woman has an unborn baby
.Pregnant .Sweet

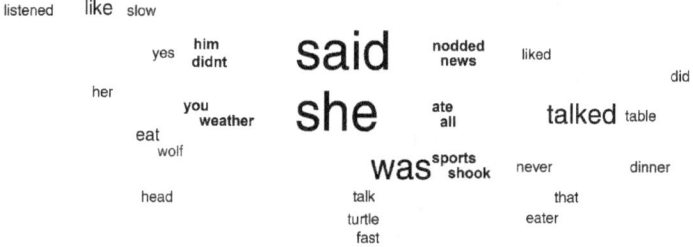

Eat Like a Wolf

She was a fast eater. She liked to eat fast. She ate like a **wolf**. "I am like a wolf," she said. He was a slow eater. He liked to eat slow. He ate like a **turtle**. "You are like a turtle," she said. She didn't talk at the dinner table. All she did was eat. He liked to talk at the dinner table. He talked about the news. He talked about the weather. He talked about sports. She listened to him talk. She **nodded** her head. That meant yes. She shook her head. That meant no. He talked. She listened. She never said yes. She never said no. She never said anything. All she did was eat.

.Wolf: A wild animal that looks like a dog

.Turtle: An animal has hard shell

.Nod: To move your head up and down
*Fast# Slow

Answer the following questions*:*
1. How was she eat?
   a. She eats fast   b. She doesn't eat quick
   c. She eats slow   d. She doesn't eat fast
2. What did he like to do at the dinner table?
   a. He liked to listen to the music
   b. He liked to watch news
   c. He liked to talked
   d. He liked to sing a song
3. What did she mean by nodding her head?
   a. She meant "Yes"   b. She meant " I'm hungry"
   c. She meant "No"   d. She meant nothing

Fill in the blank*.*
1. She ate like a ....
2. He was a .... eater.
3. He ate like a ....
4. She didn't talk at the ....
5. All she did was ....

Matching.
.Fast   .Move your head up and down
.Nod   .Slow
.Wolf   .Wild animal

About the authors
Dr Azadeh Nemati is an Assistant Professor in Iran, majoring in ELT. She is the member of *Network of Women Scientists of the Islamic world* and also the editor in chief of some international journals. She has already published + 15 books and + 30 articles nationally and internationally. She has presented in many international conferences and also supervised some MA theses. In 2010, 2012 and 2014 she was selected as distinguished researcher in the University. Her main area of interest includes:
   TESL, TEFL, Sociolinguistics, Language Learning and Teaching, Vocabulary Learning and Teaching, Strategies, Gender Studies, Translation studies.
Other books of this writer are available at her website: www.BaNarvan.com
Respected readers can reach her at BaNarvan@gmail.com

Marjan Khoshparvar has been teaching since 1392. She is interested to teach and interact with students and deal with children and teenagers in a friendly manner. At present, she is studying MA of English Teaching at Shiraz Azad University. She has got her B.A in English translation.
Respected readers can reach her at Marrjan.kh@gmail.com

www.ingramcontent.com/pod-product-compliance
Lightning Source LLC
Chambersburg PA
CBHW051713090426
42736CB00013B/2693